South American Animals

# Jaguars

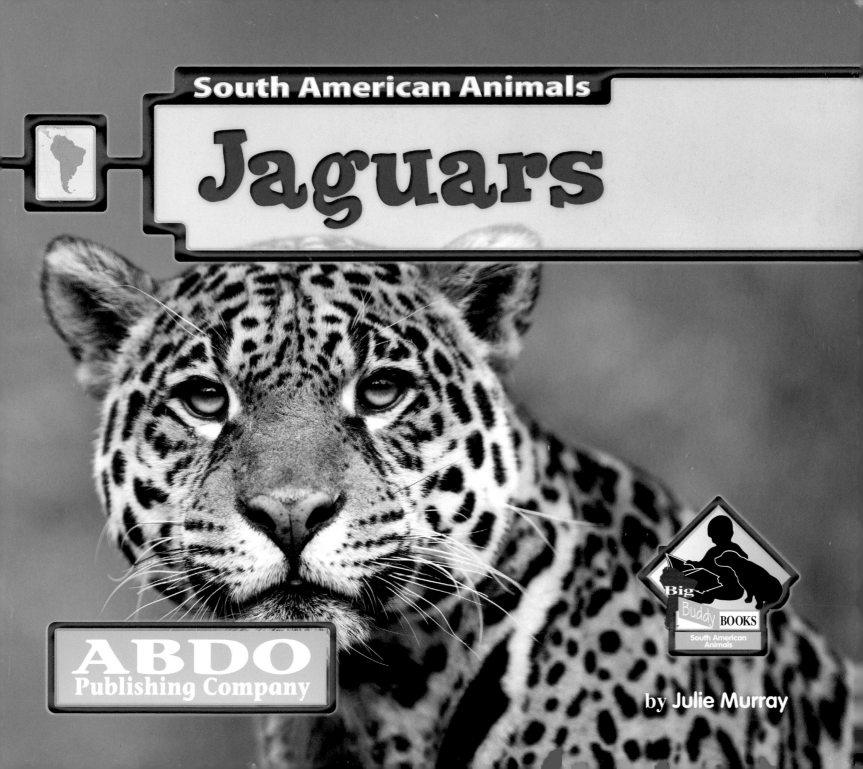

ABDO
Publishing Company

Big
Buddy BOOKS
South American
Animals

by Julie Murray

## VISIT US AT
**www.abdopublishing.com**

Published by ABDO Publishing Company, PO Box 398166, Minneapolis, Minnesota 55439.

Copyright © 2014 by Abdo Consulting Group, Inc. International copyrights reserved in all countries. No part of this book may be reproduced in any form without written permission from the publisher. Big Buddy Books™ is a trademark and logo of ABDO Publishing Company.

Printed in the United States of America, North Mankato, Minnesota.
092013
012014

♻ PRINTED ON RECYCLED PAPER

Coordinating Series Editor: Rochelle Baltzer
Editor: Marcia Zappa
Contributing Editors: Megan M. Gunderson, Sarah Tieck
Graphic Design: Maria Hosley
Cover Photograph: *iStockphoto*: ©iStockphoto.com/Palenque.
Interior Photographs/Illustrations: *Glow Images*: © Tom Brakefield/CORBIS (pp. 19, 27), Juniors Bildarchiv (pp. 13, 29), Loren McIntyre (p. 17), Mark Newman/FLPA (p. 7), Wendy Shattil (p. 5), SuperStock (pp. 8, 19, 25); *iStockphoto*: ©iStockphoto.com/andDraw (p. 9), ©iStockphoto.com/EcoVentures-Travel (p. 21), ©iStockphoto.com/RollingEarth (p. 15), ©iStockphoto.com/JohanSjolander (p. 4), ©iStockphoto.com/taraminchin (p. 15); *Minden Pictures*: ZSSD (p. 27); *Science Source*: Thomas & Pat Leeson (p. 7); *Shutterstock*: Ammit Jack (p. 4), Bedrin (p. 11), Patryk Kosmider (p. 23), Rechitan Sorin (p. 9).

### Library of Congress Cataloging-in-Publication Data

Murray, Julie, 1969-
 Jaguars / Julie Murray.
    pages cm --  (South American animals)
 Audience: Ages 7-11.
 ISBN 978-1-62403-190-8
1.  Jaguar--Juvenile literature.  I. Title.
 QL737.C23M883 2013
 599.75'5--dc23
                               2013025493

# Contents

Long ago, nearly all land on Earth was one big mass. About 200 million years ago, the land began to break into **continents**. One of these is South America.

Jaguars are the largest cats in North and South America.

South America includes several countries and **cultures**. It is known for its rain forests and interesting animals. One of these animals is the jaguar.

# Jaguar Territory

Jaguars are found in South America, Mexico, and Central America. Central America is the southern part of North America.

Jaguars live in many types of **habitats**. These include rain forests, grasslands, woodlands, and swamps. Jaguars are almost always found near water.

Jaguar Territory

Unlike most cats, jaguars like water. They are strong swimmers. They can even hunt while swimming. And, they often take a dip to cool off on hot days.

Jaguars usually live in areas with lots of plants. That way, they can hide while hunting.

# Welcome to South America!

If you took a trip to where jaguars live, you might find…

## …wet weather.

South America is home to the world's largest tropical rain forest. The Amazon is in northern South America. It receives about 60 to 175 inches (152 to 445 cm) of rain each year!

## ...flat land.

Many jaguars are found in the Central Plains. This large, flat area covers the center of South America. It has grassland, tropical rain forest, and woodland areas.

## ...different countries.

Twelve countries make up South America. Each has its own history and cultures. Brazil (*flag at left*) is the largest in area and population. Argentina is the second largest in area. Colombia is the second largest in population.

# Take a Closer Look

Jaguars are members of the cat family. They have strong bodies and legs. A jaguar's large head has furry ears, light eyes, and round cheeks. Its **snout** has a dark nose and powerful square **jaws**.

Adult jaguars have yellowish or golden eyes. They see well at night.

Adult jaguars grow up to 30 inches (76 cm) tall at their shoulders. They are 3.5 to 6 feet (1 to 2 m) long. Their tails are another 17 to 36 inches (43 to 91 cm) long. Adult jaguars weigh 70 to more than 300 pounds (32 to more than 136 kg).

**Uncovered!**

Jaguars vary in size based on their habitat. Jaguars that live in thick forests tend to be smaller than those that live in more open areas.

Jaguars are the third-largest type of cat in the world. Only lions and tigers are bigger.

# Seeing Spots

Jaguars are known for their spotted coats. Most have a base coat of tan, gold, or orange fur. White or light yellow fur covers the cheeks, throat, and belly. Some have a base coat of reddish brown or black fur.

A jaguar's spots are solid black on its head and neck. Larger spots called rosettes cover its back and sides. Each rosette has a group of black spots around a dark center. There is a small black spot in the middle.

**Uncovered!**
A jaguar's spots are called rosettes because they are shaped like roses.

A black jaguar's spots may be hard to see. But, they are noticeable up close. Black jaguars are often found in thick forest habitats.

A jaguar's spots help it hide among plants while hunting.

# Mighty Hunters

Jaguars are **carnivores**. They eat many different types of **prey**. These include large animals such as deer, tapirs, pig-like peccaries, and alligator-like caimans. Jaguars also eat smaller animals such as porcupines, sloths, snakes, and fish.

16

Jaguars eat more than 85 different types of prey!

A jaguar often drags its prey to a hidden spot to eat.

Jaguars hunt alone. They usually hunt at night or near sunrise or sunset. Sometimes, a jaguar hides and waits for its **prey** to come close. Other times, it creeps toward it.

When prey is close, a jaguar **pounces** on it. It can kill by biting its prey's neck. Or, it can use its strong **jaws** to crush its prey's skull. A jaguar is the only type of cat that has a bite powerful enough to do this.

Jaguars mostly hunt on the ground. But, sometimes they climb trees to pounce on their prey from above!

# Independent Life

Adult jaguars generally live alone. Each one has a home area. Often, a male's home area overlaps with the home areas of several females. But, males and females only come together for short times to **mate**.

Jaguars don't build lasting homes. They rest in caves, under thick plants, or by large rocks.

A jaguar's home area is about 10 to 53 square miles (26 to 137 sq km). Jaguars mark their home areas by scratching trees. They also mark areas with their waste. They roar to warn others to stay away.

A jaguar's roar sounds like a low grunt. A male's roar is usually louder than a female's.

# Jaguar Babies

Jaguars are **mammals**. Females have one to four babies at a time. Most often, they have twins.

Baby jaguars are called cubs. At birth, they weigh one and a half to two pounds (0.7 to 0.9 kg). Newborn cubs are blind and helpless. They count on their mother for care.

**Uncovered!**
Jaguar mothers guard their babies closely. They do not let other animals near, even the father.

A jaguar mother gently carries her cubs in her mouth.

Jaguar cubs drink their mother's milk for about five to six months. As they grow, they begin to eat meat from her **prey**.

Jaguar cubs learn to hunt by watching their mother. After one to two and a half years, they are ready to live on their own.

Cubs are curious and playful. They chase each other and pretend to fight.

# Survivors

Life in South America isn't easy for jaguars. They have no natural predators. But, people kill them for their spotted coats. Ranchers kill them to keep them from hunting cattle. And, much of their **habitat** has been lost to logging, buildings, and farms.

Still, jaguars **survive**. Many countries have laws against killing them. And, people are working to save their habitats. Jaguars help make South America an amazing place.

**Uncovered!**
Jaguars are near threatened. This means
they are in a little danger of dying out.

# Wow!

## I'll bet you never knew...

...that the name *jaguar* means "animal that kills with one leap." It comes from the native word *yaguara*.

...that jaguars are one of only four types of cats that can roar! Only members of the *Panthera* group of cats share this special talent. This includes lions, tigers, and leopards.

...that there is no such cat as a black panther. *Panther* is a word used for big cats. So, a cat that someone might call a black panther is really just a black jaguar, leopard, or puma.

...that jaguars were important to many native **cultures**. They often stood for power and courage. Some cultures considered the animal a god.

# Important Words

**carnivore** (KAHR-nuh-vawr) an animal or a plant that eats meat.

**continent** one of Earth's seven main land areas.

**culture** (KUHL-chuhr) the arts, beliefs, and ways of life of a group of people.

**habitat** a place where a living thing is naturally found.

**jaws** a mouthpart that allows for holding, crushing, and chewing.

**mammal** a member of a group of living beings. Mammals make milk to feed their babies and usually have hair or fur on their skin.

**mate** to join as a couple in order to reproduce, or have babies.

**pounce** to dive down on and seize something.

**prey** an animal hunted or killed by a predator for food.

**snout** a part of the face, including the nose and the mouth, that sticks out. Some animals, such as jaguars, have a snout.

**survive** to continue to live or exist.

# Web Sites

To learn more about jaguars, visit ABDO Publishing Company online. Web sites about jaguars are featured on our Book Links page. These links are routinely monitored and updated to provide the most current information available.

## www.abdopublishing.com

# Index